Sacrifice.

Costly Grace and
Glorious Privilege

Simon Guillebaud

Published by 10Publishing, a division of 10ofthose.com <http://10ofthose.com>
9D Centurion Court, Farington, Leyland, PR25 3UQ, England
Email: info@10ofthose.com
Website: www.10ofthose.com <http://www.10ofthose.com>

A catalogue record for this book is available from the British Library.
ISBN: 978-1-909611-17-7

Cover Design and Typeset by: Mike Thorpe / www.design-chapel.com

Printed and bound by CPI Group (UK) Ltd, Croydon, CR0 4YY

Acknowledgements

Many areas of this book have been influenced by godly men and women who have gone before, and have written more comprehensively on the topic of sacrifice.

In places, the author's material deliberately has echoes of their work and teaching.

We acknowledge their helpful contributions.

Contents.

Show me the way of the cross once again
Denying myself for the love that I've gained
Everything's You now, everything's changed,
It's time You had my whole life;
You can have it all.

Yes, I resolve to give it all;
Some things must die,
Some things must live.
Not, 'What can I gain,'
But, 'What can I give?'
If much is required when much is received,
Then You can have my whole life;
Jesus, have it all.

I've given like a beggar but lived like the rich
And crafted myself a more comfortable cross,
Yet what I am called to is deeper than this,
It's time You had my whole life;
You can have it all.

(Matt Redman, 'The Way of the Cross' from the album
The Friendship and the Fear, Star Song Music, 1998)

Introduction.

Matt Redman's song speaks of us crafting ourselves a more comfortable cross. However, a comfortable cross simply doesn't make sense. There was never anything comfortable about a cross. As words, comfort and cross cannot coherently co-exist. They are irreconcilable. The cross – Christianity's universally recognized symbol – represents sacrifice, excruciating pain and death. Subsequently, the resurrection represents hope and victory. And so it is rightly said that the cross we bear precedes the crown we wear. That order is very important to remember.

What you have in front of you is a call to sacrifice. Sacrifice is a huge topic, but this book is intentionally short so we will not be able to look at it in great depth. I was asked to write a book on this theme and thought long and hard about it. My hesitation lay in the fact that my sacrifices for Christ have been relatively small. You might consider them more substantial as I share some of my own personal journey in these coming pages, but honestly, I know how much the Lord has called me to lay down so far and there are many, many people who are more qualified than me to write out of the depths and pain of their personal experiences with and for Jesus.

And indeed even those things that are often thought of as sacrifices I consider privileges. Can something be called a sacrifice if it is simply giving back to God a small part of the debt that we owe? Is it a sacrifice to spend time working with other Christians spreading the good news of Jesus and, in doing so, being constantly focused on the bright hope of being with Him after this life? I'd rather say it's not a sacrifice but a privilege.

I want to emphasize this more. It is critical that we think of privilege and sacrifice going hand in hand. Whereas 'comfortable' and 'cross' don't sit well together, 'privilege' and 'sacrifice' do, for the authentic follower of Christ. We must agree on that, because otherwise the whole concept sounds grim, daunting and negative.

What inspired me to lay my life down for the cause of Christ was, in large part, reading about other men and women across the centuries who 'did not love their lives so much as to shrink from death' (Rev. 12:11). Their example set the standard in terms of what should be a normative response to God's call on our lives. It just seemed logical to me that if Jesus, who is God, died for me, then no sacrifice can be too great for me to make for Him.

If Jesus, who is God, died for me, then no sacrifice can be too great for me to make for Him.

So, as we take a short look at what sacrifice involves for the follower of Jesus, I make no apology for giving plenty of examples from the lives of the saints of yesteryear as well as quoting their words, because there is an authenticity and authority behind such actions and pronouncements that I simply cannot claim to have fully experienced and lived out.

Their words and deeds will inspire you more than mine. And inspiration is what I'm shooting for in these pages. If you get to the end of them and are more fired up to aim higher, go deeper, and reach further in your love and pursuit of Christ, then this book will have done its job.

As we consider five aspects of Christian sacrifice we'll use what the apostle Paul says in Romans 12:1 as our springboard.

> Therefore, I urge you, brothers, in view of God's mercy, to offer your bodies as living sacrifices, holy and pleasing to God – this is your spiritual act of worship.

God give us ears to hear, eyes to see, discerning minds, and hearts committed to enact His call to be a living sacrifice!

Simon Guillebaud, July 2013

Grace-full Sacrifice.

Therefore, I urge you, brothers, in view of God's mercy, to offer your bodies as living sacrifices, holy and pleasing to God – this is your spiritual act of worship.

Sacrifice is all about grace. Paul knew that. Having pursued and murdered Christians in his misguided zeal to wipe out any trace of this subversive new sect, he had plenty of blood on his hands. But that blood-guilt was washed away through the very blood of the One whose followers he had hunted down. And, after that, everything changed. It was no longer about rituals and regulations; now it was about relationship. It was no longer suffocating and oppressive, but liberating and exciting. It was no longer external performance, but inward reality. It was no longer confined to the few, but it was open to everyone. That's where Romans 12:1 picks it up.

In the previous two chapters, Paul has been expounding this truly revolutionary concept, that everyone has access to the grace of God – not just the Jewish nation, but everyone. So he bursts into a spontaneous song of praise at the end of chapter 11, and then launches into chapter 12. Sacrifice springs from grace. Paul's writings are saturated in it. He says, 'Therefore . . . in view of God's mercy'. God's 'mercy' should really read 'mercies'. The original Greek word is plural. I often go through all His mercies to me. I do this all the more because of an experience I had a few years ago, when a man I'd been helping in Burundi turned nasty. He came to my house with a grenade to kill me, and wrote a letter saying he was going to cut out my eyes.

I know that the call of God will never take me where the grace of God will not keep me.

It wasn't a pleasant experience, but it made me thankful for the mercy of sight for the first time in my life. Previously I had always taken the gift of sight for granted. I thought it was a right. But no, sight is a gift – as are so many other things we can so easily take for granted, such as health, food, clean water, electricity, freedom to worship, safety, education, peace and a whole lot more. From that day I have lived a much more grateful life. This verse has become deeply embedded as a core life principle. Everything is a gift. My sacrifice for Jesus, whatever it looks like, springs out of His mercies to me. I know that the call of God will never take me where the grace of God will not keep me.

I don't know what the Lord is calling you to, but I know that grateful people are joyful people. Psalm 100:2 encourages us to 'Serve the Lord with gladness' (NKJV). Obedient sacrifice comes out of worship to God. God does not require unwilling helpers. Joyfulness in service to God is like oil on a bicycle chain. Without it we become weary and slow. Again: God does not require unwilling helpers. The angels in heaven, in their service to God, don't drag their feet and grumble and moan and say, 'Why me?' If we want to model obedience – if we want to model grace – it's critical that in our service to God we get the root motivation right.

Embracing the call to sacrifice may sound heroic and unattainable, but that isn't the case. It's recognizing God for who He is, and living consistently with that reality. The invitation isn't limited to spiritual giants. On the contrary, 'God's giants have been weak men who did great things for God because they reckoned on His being with them', as the missionary Hudson Taylor once said. What they were counting on was God's faithfulness. Sacrifice is invariably mundane and totally unglamorous. It has been inbred in us that we have to *do* exceptional things for God. But we don't. We have to *be* exceptional in the ordinary things. That might mean sticking it out in a horrible job, offering forgiveness to someone who's not even sorry, giving time or finances at great personal cost, or letting go of our right to get even. These things are all challenges, and fly in the face of today's tendency to lower the bar – settling for a diluted call to holiness, and embracing a comfortable cross on our own terms. The result is exchanging God's glorious grace for a debased cheapened version.

> **If we want to model obedience it's critical that in our service to God we get the root motivation right.**

Dietrich Bonhoeffer wrote of this in his classic *The Cost of Discipleship*.[1] He notes that many Christians 'have gathered like ravens around the carcass of cheap grace and there have drunk the poison which has killed the following of Christ.' He elaborates on this theme:

Cheap grace is the preaching of forgiveness without requiring repentance, baptism without church discipline, communion without confession, absolution without personal confession. Cheap grace is grace without discipleship, grace without the cross, grace without Jesus Christ, living and incarnate.

Costly grace is the treasure hidden in the field; for the sake of it a man will gladly go and sell all that he has. It is the pearl of great price to buy which the merchant will sell all his goods. It is the kingly rule of Christ, for whose sake a man will pluck out the eye which causes him to stumble; it is the call of Jesus Christ at which the disciple leaves his nets and follows Him.

Costly grace is the gospel which must be sought again and again, the gift which must be asked for, the door at which a man must knock.

Such grace is costly because it calls us to follow, and it is grace because it calls us to follow Jesus Christ. It is costly because it costs a man his life, and it is grace because it gives a man the only true life. It is costly because it condemns sin, and grace because it justifies the sinner. Above all, it is costly because it cost God the life of His Son: 'ye were bought at a price', and what has cost God much cannot be cheap for us. Above all, it is grace because God did not reckon His Son too dear a price to pay for our

> life, but delivered Him up for us. Costly grace is the Incarnation of God.

We must listen to Paul the first-century martyr and to Bonhoeffer the twentieth-century one, and recognize the costly call to surrender and the potential consequences of a life offered up as a living sacrifice. Both were wholehearted and willing to lay their lives down because of their understanding of God's grace imparted to them. Both trusted implicitly in God's loving character. Both considered all other worldly achievements rubbish compared to the surpassing greatness of knowing Christ Jesus as Lord. There are many other examples throughout history of people embracing this challenge. Are we prepared to be in their number?

NOTE

1. Dietrich Bonhoeffer, *The Cost of Discipleship* (NY: Touchstone, 1995).

Urgent Sacrifice.

Therefore, I urge you, brothers, in view of God's mercy, to offer your bodies as living sacrifices, holy and pleasing to God – this is your spiritual act of worship.

In calling us to offer our bodies as living sacrifices, Paul doesn't simply encourage us, or suggest it might be a good idea – he *urges* us. Why? Because there is an urgent need for God's people, in light of His mercy, to please Him.

Ambushes were commonplace during my early years in Burundi. They were an easy way of instilling fear over a whole region. In one such ambush the rebels ordered everyone out of the bus. In what would seem comical, but for the seriousness of what was going on, two people managed to dive into the ditch on the side of the road without the rebels spotting them. One was a huge middle-aged lady. The other, lying face-to-face on top of her in a seemingly highly compromising position, was a pastor. As the rebels lined up the passengers and shot them one by one in the head, the pastor whispered to the lady, 'You need to receive Jesus into your heart right now, because we're going to die, and you need to know where you're going.' Mercifully, they survived to tell the tale.

On another occasion, I was at a crowded meeting near the Congolese border, on a makeshift stage under the blistering heat of the ascending sun. My sermon text was Matthew 25 – the parable of the ten maidservants. In Jesus' story, all of them had been invited to the wedding celebration. However, the bridal party was late. All nodded off as night fell, but then the call came: the bridegroom was soon to arrive. So the maidservants trimmed their lamps to get ready. As we know, five maidservants were ready, the other five were not; the latter had to run off and buy some more oil, during which time the bridegroom arrived. Those who were ready went with him to the wedding celebrations. The door was then shut, definitively. Those who were late arrived eventually, but were told, 'I tell you the truth, I don't know you' (Matt. 25:12).

It's a straightforward story, and it doesn't need much explaining. My three points were simply:

1. Jesus is coming.

2. Nobody knows when.

3. Are you ready?

A number of people responded to the invitation. Plenty of others declined. Perhaps some thought they'd respond and get themselves ready for next week, or next year. In any case, two days later I was driving towards their village on my motorbike only to be turned back by a group of soldiers, as killing was taking place up ahead in a rebel attack. An undisclosed number died and it struck me as never before just how urgent a message we have been entrusted with. How many of those who died had accepted or declined the invitation just forty-eight hours earlier? God knows. For each of those people unfortunate enough to be caught in the crossfire, their time to meet Jesus had come. They hadn't known when, but the most important issue remained – were they ready?

Clearly, neither of the above examples are scenarios familiar to many of us. But the same sense of urgency is called for in our respective circumstances if we really understand what's going on around us. The stakes are very high. These days most of us show by our priorities and approach to spiritual things that we believe we are in peacetime. But we're not. We are engaged in a spiritual war and we must be on the alert. We must be armed. We must be vigilant. Think about it: casualties in this war don't merely lose an arm or an eye or even their physical life, but they lose everything, and face eternal separation from God.

> These days most of us show by our priorities and approach to spiritual things that we believe we are in peacetime.

On 4th July 1854, a well-known criminal by the name of Charlie Peace was hanged in London. As he was marched to the gallows, an accompanying priest read from the liturgy. 'Those who die without Christ experience hell which is the pain of forever dying without the release which death itself can bring.' Charlie stopped in his tracks and confronted the priest. 'Do you believe that? Do you honestly believe what you just read out to me?' The priest was flustered. He said, 'Well, I suppose, yes, I believe so.' The criminal replied, 'Well, I don't, but if I did, I'd get down on my hands and knees and crawl all over Britain, even if it were paved with broken glass, if I could just rescue one person.'

Whatever the current controversies about the reality of hell and what it looks like, suffice to say the picture painted in the Bible is unimaginably grim, and Jesus and the apostles in their writings didn't shy away from addressing it. Jesus said, 'Whoever believes in the Son has eternal life, but whoever rejects the Son will not see life, for God's wrath remains on him' (John 3:36). In 2 Thessalonians 1:8,9, Paul wrote, 'He will punish those who do not know God and do not obey the gospel of our Lord Jesus. They will be punished with everlasting destruction and shut out from the presence of the Lord and from the majesty of his power'.

Such verses inspired generations of missionaries to take the gospel to the four corners of the globe, to risk indescribable suffering, and to lay down their lives as living sacrifices. John Paton travelled with his family to the New Hebrides islands, where, within a short period of time, his wife and baby died. Yet he was able to declare, 'When the island of Tanna turns to the Lord and is won for Christ, men in years after will find the memory of that spot still green, where, with ceaseless prayers and tears, I claimed that land for God in which I had buried my dead wife and baby child with faith and hope.'

Robert Jermain Thomas felt God's call to penetrate Korea with the gospel in 1866, following a massacre of about eight thousand local believers by the antagonistic regime. He boarded a US trading vessel and sailed up to Pyongyang.

Despite repeated warnings to turn back, they kept going until they were stranded on a sandbank. The Koreans set fire to their ship, at which point all the other men on board tried to escape, but were killed by soldiers on the riverbank. Thomas alone remained on board, and he threw all the Bibles he'd brought with him to those watching on the banks of the river. Eventually, he jumped into the river with his clothes ablaze. Reaching the bank, he begged a soldier to receive his last Bible as a gift. The soldier hesitated, but then fulfilled his duty by thrusting his lance through the 27-year-old Welshman. Those present were deeply impacted by the scene. Some of the Bibles were rescued and the pages used as wallpaper in people's houses. Within a short period, though, curiosity grabbed them. They began reading the Scriptures and became Christians, despite the massive personal cost that conversion brought them. One young man's life, lived and laid down with such urgency, had led to the expansion of God's fledgling kingdom in that land.

> One young man's life, lived and laid down with such urgency, had led to the expansion of God's fledgling kingdom in that land.

Be it overseas or in our own country, we need to embrace a similar sense of urgency and passion for the lost. Robert Murray M'Cheyne was another young man who died in his prime, aged 29, but not before shaking his beloved Scotland. Many people wanted to know the secret behind his spiritual power. One such enquirer embarked on a pilgrimage to M'Cheyne's church, and asked the sexton, 'Would you mind telling me what was the secret behind Robert Murray M'Cheyne's work?' So the sexton led him into M'Cheyne's former study, and invited him to sit in the great man's chair. The sexton then said plainly, 'Now drop your head on that book and weep because that's what he always did before he preached.'

The needs are everywhere. The call is to everyone. As William Booth, founder of the Salvation Army declared,

> 'Not called!' did you say? 'Not heard the call,' I think you should say. Put your ear down to the Bible and hear Him bid you go and pull sinners out of the fire of sin. Put your ear down to the burdened, agonized heart of humanity and listen to its pitiful wail for help. Go stand by the gates of hell and hear the damned entreat you to go to their father's house and bid their brothers and sisters and servants and masters not to come there. Then look Christ in the face – whose mercy you have professed to obey – and tell Him whether you will join heart and soul and body and circumstances in the march to publish His mercy to the world.

It is so easy to just cruise along in life largely apathetic and disengaged from the spiritual needs, let alone the physical needs, of those we come into contact with. Because most people don't live in a literal war zone, there is little sense of urgency to share the gospel. We don't want to risk treading on toes, offending, getting rebuffed or rejected, and we fall for one of Satan's greatest lies: don't worry about it, leave it for now, there is always time.

I came across the following obituary a number of years ago:

> Died: Salvador Sanchez, 23, World Boxing Council featherweight champion and one of the sport's best fighters; of injuries after his Porsche 928 collided with two trucks, just north of Queretaro, Mexico. A school dropout at 16, Sanchez explained, 'I found out that I liked hitting people and I didn't like school so I started boxing.' A peppery tactician, he wore opponents down for late round knockouts. His record: 43-1-1. 'I'd like to step down undefeated', he said last month. 'I'm only 23 and *I have all the time in the world.* (emphasis mine)'

He was tragically wrong. We do not have all the time in the world. My friends who died in car crashes or succumbed to cancer would not have planned things that way. How about your colleagues, loved ones, team members, neighbours? The call to sacrifice means stepping out, living urgently, and being willing to face whatever consequences might come our way.

On 19 February 1944, one of the most costly battles in the Second World War was fought at Iwo Jima. Six hundred miles south of Tokyo, its two strategic airstrips were needed by the Allies as launch pads for attacks on Japan. Twenty-two thousand Japanese soldiers knew they were there to defend to the death. About twenty-six thousand US troops died to take it. There were numerous examples of heroism amidst the bloody carnage.

It is so easy to just cruise along in life largely apathetic and disengaged from the spiritual needs.

Thousands upon thousands of men sacrificed themselves for the greater cause. If you were to visit there today, there is a message etched outside the cemetery which reads:

> When you go home
> Tell them for us and say
> For your tomorrow
> We gave our today

Paul urges us. The choice is yours. So will you, will I, give our today for others' tomorrows?

Voluntary Sacrifice.

Therefore, I urge you, brothers, in view of God's mercy, *to offer your bodies as living sacrifices*, holy and pleasing to God – this is your spiritual act of worship.

Some of you will have watched my thirteen short films on radical discipleship called *More Than Conquerors* (www.more-than-conquerors.com). One of the films involved me taking a lamb and a goat up a mountain to slaughter them as sacrifices to God. At the base of the mountain I tied some rope around each of their necks and started dragging them along with me. The purpose of the film was to show that we cannot be forced into sacrificing ourselves. It has to be, as our verse says, a free-will offering. Paul urges us 'to offer' our bodies as living sacrifices.

I used the lamb and the goat to illustrate how traditionally, when animals were sacrificed, some went willingly (the lamb), and some needed to be tied up (the goat). It soon became apparent as we headed up the mountain that I didn't need any rope for the lamb at all. I thought I'd need it to get him up the mountain when we were off camera, and then just film him without any rope. But no, he just pootled along next to me all the time whilst I had to keep on yanking the poor goat every step of the way. I won't ruin the ending for you, but it's a very powerful film. Jesus was led like a lamb to the slaughter. Not a goat, but a lamb. He was the Lamb of God who came to take away the sins of the world. Similarly we are to offer ourselves willingly to God. He won't force us. This is the purest kind of voluntary service. So in our very self-obsessed age, here's a good question: is God going to have all of me, or am I so taken up with what I want to make of my life?

John Ortberg reflects on how Western society

> "doesn't talk much about calling any more. It is more likely to think in terms of career. Yet, for many people a career becomes the altar on which they sacrifice their lives. A calling, which is something I do for God, is replaced by a career, which threatens to become my god. A career is something I choose for myself; a calling is something I receive. A career is something I do for myself; a calling is something I do for God. A career promises status, money or power; a calling generally promises difficulty and even some suffering – and the opportunity to be used by God. A career is about upward mobility; a calling generally leads to downward mobility" John Ortburg, *If You Want to Walk on Water, You've Got to Get Out of the Boat* (Grand Rapids: Zondervan, 2001)

This sounds rather dire, but only because we have our value system upside down. We must think of success not in earthly terms but in biblical terms. That is, not in accordance with society's standards, but in accordance with a grain of wheat falling to the ground and dying and becoming what it never could be if it were to exist alone.

I remember writing to someone who wanted to join me in Burundi but had reservations because of the precarious security situation. I said, 'Why be afraid if you are surrendered to God? Don't come to Burundi if you are afraid. However, if He calls, then of course He will protect and keep you as long as He wants. Don't come for spiritual tourism – you can do that in other, peaceful, African countries. Or if you don't have faith, wait a few years until it is safe, and then you can come.'

That may sound harsh, but we need to live out what we profess to believe. We will never embrace this voluntary sacrifice if we don't fully believe the verse following on from Romans 12:1: 'Then you will be able to test and approve what God's will is – *his good, pleasing and perfect will*' (v. 2, emphasis mine). If I know my heavenly Father's will is good, pleasing and perfect, I'll do anything and go anywhere for Him. Then the sacrifice becomes something wonderful. It is not like being squeezed of something we don't want to give up; it's giving, in loving honour to God, the very best thing we have.

> **If I know my heavenly Father's will is good, pleasing and perfect, I'll do anything and go anywhere for Him.**

Think of what Christ did for you. You must follow His example. He did not choose His own sacrifice. There was a time in history when God planned your salvation. Do you realize that? Do you think of the God of this universe being that personal? It was the Father's role to command and send, and it was the Son's to obey and go. He even obeyed to the point of leaving eternity and heaven in all its glory; He came to earth; He suffered under the temptations of the devil; He spent thirty-three years in a fallen world in the company of fallen men; through it all He lived a perfect life and at the end He died a perfect death. That's sacrifice. That's perfect sacrifice modelled for us. But still we say, 'I want angels. I want people better than myself. I want everything to be significantly from God, otherwise I cannot live life or do the thing properly.' No. Let God command and send, and let us obey and go. If He calls you, He is with you.

I heard of one man who was literally crushed for his belief in Jesus in Zimbabwe. He wrote the following before he was martyred:

> I'm part of the fellowship of the unashamed. I have the Holy Spirit's power. The die has been cast. I have stepped over the line. The decision has been made – I'm a disciple of His. I won't look back, let up, slow down, back away, or be still. I will not flinch in the face of sacrifice, hesitate in the presence of the enemy, pander at the pool of popularity, or meander in the maze of mediocrity. I am a disciple of Jesus. I must go until He comes, give until I drop, preach until all know, and work until He stops me. And, when He comes for His own, He will have no problem recognizing me because my banner will be clear!

God wants us to lay down willingly our desire for acceptance, approval and endorsement. We must voluntarily lay down our reputation, and be set free from the tyranny of public opinion. In the eighteenth century, the Church of England fiercely opposed all evangelicals and closed their pulpits to the likes of George Whitefield and John Wesley. There was no other option for ministers of the gospel than to take to the streets, markets and fields. Whitefield quickly understood that and embraced the cost willingly, with staggering results. Wesley didn't want to preach in the open air because he was a man of a certain standing. He went through a deep torment of soul. The idea of preaching in a field profoundly offended him, but he knew it was the only course left. A friend remonstrated with him and pleaded with him not to go ahead because it would ruin his good name, but Wesley replied, 'When I gave my all to God I did not withhold my reputation.' He took to the open air, saying: 'I consented to be more vile . . . I set myself on fire, and people came to see me burn.'

Similarly, when William Wilberforce was converted in 1785 at the age of 25, he planned to turn his back on politics and go into the ordained ministry, as he thought 'spiritual' affairs were far more important than 'secular' affairs. Thankfully, John Newton, the former slave trader, intervened and persuaded him to persevere in the political domain. 'It is hoped and believed that the Lord has raised you up for the good of the nation,' said Newton, echoing Mordecai's words to Queen Esther (Esth. 4:14). After seeking the Lord's guidance, Wilberforce consented and embarked on a lifelong campaign as a parliamentarian, speaking out against many of the social evils of the day and being used by God to bring about radical transformations with worldwide repercussions. He wrote in his journal in 1788: 'My walk is a

> Let God command and send, and let us obey and go. If He calls you, He is with you.

public one. My business is in the world; and I must mix in the assemblies of men, or quit the post which providence seems to have assigned me.'

Wilberforce knew God's call on his life was a costly one. He knew he would have to persevere for decades as he took on the likes of Admiral Lord Nelson and the interests of the royal family. He could have chosen the easier path of full-time ordained ministry. Yet he chose to reject a more comfortable "cross" and embrace his voluntary sacrifice.

Now I've shared some words from Christendom's heavyweights, and you might be objecting, saying that they were simply extraordinary men, and you could never do what they did. But listen carefully; God is not calling you to do what they did. He is calling you to be fully you. He gives us all we need to do the work He has called us to do. It's about being exceptional in the ordinary things. But the bottom line is, no matter what situation in life we find ourselves, we have to decide to be totally committed. We have to be prepared to embrace the costly adventure of being a living sacrifice. And let us not forget that if we're living sacrifices there will always be the temptation to climb off the altar when things get rough. It's a warning that if we step out of line with God's will we step into nowhere. I've been nowhere – a place of conscious disobedience to God's call – and I can tell you, it's a miserable place to be. Thank God for grace, that He brought me back, and that He'll do the same for every sincerely repentant sinner. It's all in response to His grace. It's urgent that we embrace His call. And it has to be done freely and willingly.

Holy Sacrifice.

Therefore, I urge you, brothers, in view of God's mercy, to offer your bodies as living sacrifices, *holy and pleasing to God* – this is your spiritual act of worship.

D.L. Moody was an evangelist from Chicago. He wasn't highly educated, but he had a passion for souls. Before he came to England, in the summer of 1872, he knew that he would have to shake London in order to have a fruitful time throughout the rest of the land. This was of course before the age of easy mass communication. I used to cycle across London Bridge each day on my way to Bible college and wonder how on earth you could shake London with the gospel. In a similar vein, his contemporary, Charles Spurgeon, had written, 'Give me twelve men – importunate men, lovers of souls, who fear nothing but sin and love nothing but God – and I will shake London from end to end.' At any rate, Moody did shake London – or rather, God did through Moody – and the whole of England on the back of it.

It's estimated he led a million people to Christ throughout several decades of relentless preaching on both sides of the Atlantic. On one occasion, earlier on in his life, he was talking to a man named Henry Varley. Varley said, 'You know, D.L. [as Moody was known to his friends], the world has yet to see what God will do with one man fully consecrated to Him.' Moody thought about it. 'The world has yet to see what God will do with one man. Any man? Doesn't have to have a great education? Any man? Fully consecrated to Him.' That was the condition – full consecration to the Lord. He continued to mull it over, and finally he concluded, 'By the grace of God, I'll be that man!'

Well, by the grace of God, you be that man or woman, that student, that young professional, that parent or grandparent, glorifying God in the media, or the arts, or politics, or business, or education. I don't claim to be fully consecrated to Him – that's what I'm aiming for, and it's a lifelong process only attained in glory – but I can say that we are being used to shake Burundi for His glory. I'll do it in Burundi. You do it where He's called you to be.

Jesus modelled perfect, holy living. He fully engaged with culture.

Our verse tells us that we are to be 'holy and pleasing to God'. The issue is full, undivided consecration, which means being dedicated, set apart for God. It involves surrendering our disappointments, hurts and fears, our longings, dreams and aspirations, our finances, health and hobbies, our family, friends, the lot. It includes what we eat, watch, read and value. The list goes on. Holiness encompasses everything.

Holiness is often portrayed negatively but the Bible portrays holiness as beautiful. Jesus personified holiness. He was so attractive to the masses, whilst repugnant to the proud, the self-serving, and the oppressors. Jesus modelled perfect, holy living. He fully engaged with culture. He empowered the marginalized, touched the untouchable, healed the broken and validated the disenfranchised. He denounced hypocrisy, challenged unjust oppression and showed compassion. That is what holiness means. And it's costly and painful to reach out and aspire to.

There's a story of a weekly women's Bible study group that were studying Malachi 3:3. They read, 'He will sit as a refiner and purifier of silver'. The group discussed this analogy to understand what the significance was. It seemed the Lord chooses to put His people in the furnace. The purpose is to burn off the impurities, but God watches the refining process take place.

One woman in the group was fascinated by the analogy and wanted to gain the full impact of it so she went to see a silversmith the following day. She observed him at work for a while, and then asked him, 'Do you have to sit here the whole time the refining process is taking place?' 'Yes,' he said. 'It's important. If the temperature rises by even the slightest degree, the silver will be damaged.' The woman was comforted by the thought that similarly the Lord was watching over her, and however difficult her current circumstances were, He was in control. He wouldn't let the refining process go on a minute longer than was required, because His purposes were good and He didn't want her to be damaged. After a while the woman got up to leave, but as she was halfway out the door the silversmith called her back and told her he had forgotten one detail: he only knew that the refining process was complete when he could see his own image reflected in the silver.

As already stated, this is a lifelong process. 2 Corinthians 3:18 puts it this way: 'And we all, who with unveiled faces contemplate the Lord's glory, are being transformed into his image with ever-increasing glory, which comes from the Lord, who is the Spirit' (TNIV). Our likeness to Jesus is growing day by day, but there can also be a specific definite time when we embrace total consecration. George Müller worked in Bristol caring for thousands of orphans in the nineteenth century. He was a man of intercession who saw mind-blowing daily responses to his prayers for provision, without ever asking people for money. One day he was urged to share what he considered to be the power behind his ministry. 'There was a day,' he said, 'when I utterly died.' As he spoke, he bent lower until he almost touched the floor. 'I died to George Müller, his opinions, preferences, tastes and will. I died to the world, its approval or censure. I died to the approval or blame even of my brethren and friends and since then I have studied only to show myself approved of God.'

> **Our likeness to Jesus is growing day by day, but there can also be a specific time when we embrace total consecration.**

This is something to aspire to: that above all, God would approve of our lives acted out before Him as we live only for the applause of nail-scarred hands.

Walter Lewis Wilson had a similarly defining experience to Müller's. He was an American doctor born towards the end of the nineteenth century, and a faithful Christian who often hosted missionaries visiting his church. One visitor from France, who didn't mince words, asked him, 'Who is the Holy Spirit to you?' Wilson's answer was doctrinally correct: 'One of the Persons of the Godhead: Teacher, Guide, Third Person of the Trinity.' But it was an empty and rehearsed response. The visitor pushed him harder, challenging him, 'You haven't answered my question.' Wilson opened up with real candour: 'He's nothing to me. I have no contact with Him and could get along just fine without Him.' The following year, Wilson listened to a sermon at church from the same verse we are considering in Romans 12, on the challenge to offer his body as a living sacrifice. The preacher called out from the pulpit, 'Have you noticed that this verse doesn't tell us to whom we should give our bodies? It's not the Lord Jesus. He has His own body. It's not the Father. He remains on His throne. Another has come to earth without a body. God gives you the indescribable honour of presenting your bodies to the Holy Spirit, to be His dwelling place on earth.'

Wilson was struck to the core and rushed home to seek the Lord. He fell on his face and pleaded with the Lord, 'My Lord, I've treated You like a servant. When I wanted You, I called for You. Now I give You this body from my head to my feet. I give You my hands, my limbs, my eyes and lips, my brain. You may send this body to Africa, or lay it on a bed with cancer. It's Your body from this moment on.'

The next morning, Wilson was working in his office when two women arrived, trying to sell him advertising. He immediately led them to Christ. The previous night's surrender had enabled him to access new power from on high. From that day onwards his life entered a new dimension of evangelistic fruitfulness. He went on to pioneer a church plant, a mission organization and a Bible college.

Do you want to be entrusted with that same power from the Holy Spirit? Well, who is the Holy Spirit to you? Like the early Wilson, can you get along perfectly well without Him, or are you truly willing to offer Him your body as a living sacrifice without conditions or caveats? There's so much more power that I want to plug into for God's glory, but will I trust Him for every aspect of my life? Will I consider everything a loss compared to the surpassing greatness of knowing Christ Jesus? These are big, big questions. He's inviting you to total surrender. Will you abandon everything to Jesus? If you're ready, take a few minutes reflecting on John Wesley's 'Covenant Prayer', and then make it your own.

I am no longer my own, but Yours.

Put me to what You will,

Rank me with whoever You will.

Put me to suffering.

Let me be employed for You,

Or laid aside for You.

Exalted for You,

Or brought low for You.

Let me be full,

Let me be empty.

Let me have all things,

Let me have nothing!

And now, O Father,

You are mine and I am Yours.

So be it.

And the covenant I am making on earth,

Let it be ratified in heaven.

Amen.

This call to holiness is so radically different from what most people aspire to, even in the church. We must be sure we are people who aren't concerned with happiness over holiness, with security over souls. We should always seek to serve and never to be served. So often we opt for a Christianity that costs us little. Sacrifice is not a word that is often on our lips. We emphasize our rights, not our responsibilities; our freedom in Christ, rather than our debt to Christ.

My concern in writing on this theme is that embracing the call to be a holy sacrifice might prove too daunting for us as we are challenged to lay everything down. I love that Paul writes that we are to be holy and pleasing to God. We *can* please Him. Indeed, if we're trying to please Him, He's pleased. I learned that a few years ago, as we were having visa issues after the birth of our third child. Consequently the five of us were stuck in England with my wonderful in-laws in their not so wonderful small two-bedroom apartment. It was cramped and challenging, and as weeks became months, I began to question God's guidance in our lives.

In the end we were delayed for eleven months. But once I'd learned what He wanted to teach me, it turned into the best time of our marriage thus far. Throughout the process I would repeat this prayer by Thomas Merton which often brought me to tears:

> My Lord God, I have no idea where I am going. I do not see the road ahead of me. I cannot know for certain where it will end. Nor do I really know myself and the fact that I think I am following Your will does not mean that I am actually doing so. But I believe that the desire to please You does in fact please You.

That last line blew me away. May it do the same to you. If we're giving it our best shot, despite our inadequacies and failings, our fickleness and frailties, then He's pleased with us. It doesn't mean there aren't areas of my life that might need minor tweaking or even wholesale revamping, but if I lay it all down for Him then He's pleased with me, and that brings me tremendous comfort, joy and motivation to continue His work.

Logical Sacrifice.

Therefore, I urge you, brothers, in view of
God's mercy, to offer your bodies as living
sacrifices, holy and pleasing to God – *this is your
spiritual act of worship.*

When I wrote my first book, *More Than Conquerors – A Call to Radical Discipleship*,[1] the question that underpinned it all was: how far is too far for me to go if Jesus went so far as to stretch out wide His arms on the cross for each one of us? I concluded that no sacrifice can be too great for me to make for Him.

As we draw to the end of our verse, Paul qualifies what it is to offer our bodies as living sacrifices. He writes, 'this is your spiritual act of worship.' The word for spiritual could also be translated 'reasonable' or 'thoughtful', and in the Greek is *logiken*, from which we get logical. As I seek to serve Jesus in Burundi, I am often tempted to fear or to compromise or to tone down the message, but that would be totally illogical, bearing in mind what Jesus did for me.

As I travel round the world and meet Christians of all ages from a range of backgrounds, I am saddened and sobered at the condition of many of us who profess to live by the gospel but are so marginal to the life of our societies. Even though we have been born again into a new relationship with the living God and adopted as one of His children, our lives are often still nondescript and inconsequential to those around us. Sometimes it makes me wonder if there is something wrong with the gospel. But I know that this is not the case. The gospel is wonderful – it's salvation for all those who accept it – so I conclude that the problem must lie with us Christians. Now, I'm speaking to myself as much as anyone; you're still reading this so I know that you don't want to be marginal or nondescript in your society; therefore this is a challenge that has to be taken on the chin.

In 1 Corinthians 15:19, Paul writes, 'If in Christ we have hope in this life only, we are of all people most to be pitied' (ESV). The whole of chapter 15 is discussing Christ's resurrection and its implications. If Christ's resurrection is false and the cross was His ultimate defeat, then we are pitifully delusional. Indeed, we are completely wasting our lives. But – glorious but – if He is who He claimed to be, then He's truly worth giving our all for.

In the early twentieth century in Togo, West Africa, some pioneer missionaries were holding an evangelistic outreach in the Togolese backwaters. On the first night of their preaching, a destitute peasant woman was powerfully impacted and decided to surrender her life to Christ. As was the cultural custom, each subsequent evening, those touched by the message would bring gifts of yam or maize and lay them on the altar at the front in gratitude to God. This woman was so poor that she had nothing to bring each evening, although she desperately longed to show how grateful she was. However, on the last night of the week's outreach, she came forward in the throng and triumphantly placed a silver coin on the altar. It was worth a dollar, which was a significant sum in those days. The missionary in charge saw her and feared that she had stolen it, but not wanting to embarrass her in public, waited until after the meeting had finished before he approached her and asked her how she could have afforded the gift. Eyes beaming, she replied that she was so happy to be free from her crippling guilt, to know where she was headed, and to discover the depth of the love Jesus had for her, that she wanted to contribute to making Jesus known to others who had not yet heard. She had considered it a privilege to go to a nearby plantation owner and sell herself as a slave for life for that silver coin. That was the gift she had laid on the altar that night.

If in Christ we have hope in this life only, we are of all people most to be pitied.

About the same time, a young American called William Borden felt the call of God on his life to go to China. He was an undergraduate student at Yale University and came from an affluent family. His prospects were fantastic, and a successful career would surely follow in whichever field he chose. So his family and friends were horrified when he gave up everything to become a missionary in China. They told him, 'If you want to do good things then there are plenty of needs here. Don't waste your life in a foreign country.' But despite their remonstrations he knew what he had to do. He was full of faith and hope, and boarded a ship for China. However, by the time he'd reached Egypt, cerebral meningitis had taken hold and it was clear that he was a dying man. It was at this point that he might have slipped into self-pitying despair. Thoughts could have entered his mind such as, 'What a waste of my life. They were right. I should have stayed back home, lived a respectable life and enjoyed my family and friends.' But no, as he lay dying in the port of Suez, he scribbled a brief note to his loved ones in America that made a powerful epitaph – just six words: 'No reserve, no retreat, no regrets.'

I find such stories deeply inspiring. These heroes of the faith were people like you and me who caught a glimpse of the majesty of God and knew that nothing else was worth living for. We might dismiss them as way out of our league, but they're not. God can achieve His purposes with or without human power and resources. All through history He has chosen to use nobodies because their unusual dependence on Him makes possible the unique display of His power and grace.

What a privilege that any of us, in any capacity, at any time, in any place, can serve the King of kings!

Oswald Chambers died of a ruptured appendix, aged 43, whilst serving the Lord in Egypt as a chaplain in the First World War. He said, 'If you have to calculate what you are willing to give up for Jesus Christ never say that you love Him. Jesus Christ asks us to give up the best we have got to Him, our right to ourselves.'

What a privilege that any of us, in any capacity, at any time, in any place, can serve the King of kings! When you're tempted to think of God's work as a hardship, remember David Livingstone's words: 'If a commission by an earthly king is considered an honour, how can a commission by a heavenly King be considered a sacrifice?' So often we seek a more comfortable cross; we settle for respectable religion; a pale diluted distortion of true authentic discipleship. Many loved ones will counsel us to tone it down, but that's the worst position to be in. They tell you that you shouldn't give everything. 'Give something,' they might say. 'But not everything. Not all your money. Not all your gifts or your time or your energy. Don't give your political or religious freedoms. Give *something*, but don't give everything.' They are well meaning, but sadly far from the mark of Paul's idea of a sacrificial Christian. They think that if you give everything you'll lose it, but it's the other way around; they lose because they don't give everything.

There's a story of a Christian businessman who was travelling through Korea. While passing a field, he saw a young man pulling a simple plough helped by an old man who was holding the handles. The amused businessman took a picture of the scene. 'I suppose these people are very poor,' he said to the missionary who was showing them around. The missionary said, 'Yes, those two men happen to be Christians. When their church was being built, they were keen to give something towards it, but they didn't have any money. So they decided to sell their one and only ox and give the proceeds to the church. This spring they are pulling the plough themselves.' The businessman was silent for a moment. Then he said, 'That must have been a real sacrifice.' But the missionary answered, 'They did not call it that. They thought themselves fortunate that they had an ox to sell.'

In Burundi, the second poorest country in the world, I'm being constantly humbled by people's generosity. What is logical in terms of our giving? Is it logical to store up for ourselves treasures on earth, 'where moth and rust destroy, and where thieves break in and steal', or is it logical to store up treasures in heaven? Jesus says where your treasure is, so will your heart be also (Matt. 6:19–21). The last thing I want to do is to get to the end of my life and realize that I have accumulated wealth or status or some kind of legacy, but sit there with a shrivelled soul.

The point behind a tithe is that it costs you. Thank God that Jesus didn't tithe His blood!

Could we follow John Wesley's example by setting a cap on our lifestyles? Why not? Why spend money that sometimes we don't even have on things we don't need to impress people we don't even like? Wesley modelled a beautifully different way. He worked out how much he needed to live on, and stuck to that. So when his income did increase he was simply able to give more away. Towards the end of his life, he wasn't tithing but giving away 90 per cent.

The point behind a tithe is that it costs you. Thank God that Jesus didn't tithe His blood! In the West we often struggle to identify how we can take up our crosses. One very real area is in our financial giving. Give until it hurts and see how God's favour will rest on you, because as you sow, so you will reap. God is a lavishly extravagantly generous God. He loves us and longs to show us more of Himself. I write this having experienced countless examples of Him returning what I've sown and multiplying it many times over.

If all this is true, then there must be consequences for our own lives. Where are the young men and women who will hold themselves to be something cheap in comparison to God's work? Where are those who will live their lives for Christ's sake? Where are those who will live dangerously and be reckless in His service? Where are those who love Him and the souls of men more than their own reputation? Where are the men and women who say, 'No' to self and take up Christ's cross and bear it? Where are those who are willing to be nailed to it at university or the office or the home or out on the mission field? Where are the men and women of vision today? Where are the men and women of prayer? Where are those that count God's word more important than their daily food? Where are those that have seen the King in His beauty and count all else rubbish compared with showing others who He is? Where are the adventurers and explorers who judge one human soul more valuable than a country's border? Where are God's men and women in this day of His power? Look around. Can you see it happening? Are these people around you? If not, then it must fall on you to put your ear to God's word and hear Him call, and in response echo the prophet Isaiah's words, 'Here am I. Send me!' (Isa. 6:8)

NOTE

1. Simon Guillebaud, *More Than Conquerors: A Call to Radical Discipleship* (Oxford: Monarch Books, 2010).

Conclusion.

Thousands of people will read these pages. If just a few dozen of us buy into the challenges, the world will be changed as a result. I firmly believe that heaven and earth are on tiptoe, waiting for the emergence of a movement of Spirit-led, fearless disciples. All of creation is watching expectantly for the springing up of a disciplined, freely gathered, martyr people who know in this life the power of the kingdom of God. It has happened before and it can happen again.

May it happen soon! Are you in? If so, why not start with A.W. Tozer's prayer of commitment below? See you on the battlefield somewhere and sometime; or if not, then in glory eventually. Maybe we'll recognize each other by the scars.

I come to You today, O Lord,

To give up my rights,

To lay down my life,

To offer my future,

To give my devotion, my skills, my energies.

I shall not waste time

Deploring my weaknesses

Nor my unfittedness for the work.

I acknowledge Your choice with my life

To make Your Christ attractive and intelligible

To those around me.

I come to You for spiritual preparation.

Put Your hand upon me,

Anoint me with the oil of the One with Good News.

Save me from compromise,

Heal my soul from small ambitions,

Deliver me from the itch to always be right,

Save me from wasting time.

I accept hard work, I ask for no easy place,

Help me not to judge others who walk a smoother path.

Show me those things that diminish spiritual power in a soul.

I now consecrate my days to You,

Make Your will more precious than anybody or anything.

Fill me with Your power

And when at the end of life's journey I see You face to face

May I hear those undeserved words

'Well done, you good and faithful servant.'

I ask this not for myself

But for the glory of the name of Your Son.

Amen.

Great Lakes Outreach.

A few years ago, I set up Great Lakes Outreach (GLO), which works in partnership with several organizations in the Great Lakes region of Central Africa, notably in Burundi. Its purpose is to respond to the area's massive needs and the huge potential impact of strategic involvement in cooperation with key Burundian partners.

The main areas of GLO's involvement include:

- **Evangelism and discipleship through schools and churches**

- **Printing of teaching materials**

- **Fighting the AIDS pandemic**

- **Helping to sustain an orphanage**

- **Equipping and encouraging informed dialogue between Christians and Muslims**

- **Training university students in outreach**

- **Small business development opportunities to enable income generation and self-sustainability**

All proceeds from the sale of this book will go to the work of GLO. I would love you to get involved in what the Lord is doing out in Burundi, so do get in touch by contacting info@greatlakesoutreach.org or visit our website: www.greatlakesoutreach.org. There are opportunities to come out on short-term teams, to contribute financially, to become a regional representative, and to subscribe for more detailed and personal prayer information. I look forward to hearing from you.

Simon Guillebaud

Other books by Simon include:

More than Conquerors – A Call to Radical Sacrifice (with DVD)

Dangerously Alive – African Adventures of Faith under Fire

Bike for Burundi – Riding across one Country for the Future of Another (with DVD)

All are available from www.more-than-conquerors.com

Follow Simon on Twitter: @SimonGuillebaud

Publishing

a division of **10**of those.com

10Publishing is the publishing house of **10ofthose.com**
It is committed to producing quality Christian
resources that are biblical and accessible.

www.10ofthose.com is our online retail arm selling
thousands of quality books at discounted prices.
We also service many church bookstalls
and can help your church to set up a bookstall.
Single and bulk purchases welcome.

For information contact: **sales@10ofthose.com**
or check out our website: **www.10ofthose.com**